BABOONS

Katherine Walden

PowerKiDS
press

New York

Published in 2009 by The Rosen Publishing Group, Inc.
29 East 21st Street, New York, NY 10010

First Edition

Editor: Amelie von Zumbusch
Book Design: Erica Clendening
Layout Design: Julio Gil
Photo Researcher: Jessica Gerweck

Photo Credits: Cover, pp. 5, 7, 9, 11, 13, 15, 17, 21, 23, 24 (top right, bottom left, bottom right) Shutterstock.com; pp. 19, 24 (top left) © iStockphoto.com/Barkley Fahnestock.

Library of Congress Cataloging-in-Publication Data

Walden, Katherine.
  Baboons / Katherine Walden.— 1st ed.
     p. cm. — (Safari animals)
  Includes index.
  ISBN-13: 978-1-4358-2689-2 (library binding) — ISBN 978-1-4358-3063-9 (pbk.)
  ISBN 978-1-4358-3075-2 (6-pack)
  1. Baboons—Juvenile literature. I. Title.
  QL737.P93W35 2009
  599.8'65—dc22
                              2008019532

Manufactured in the United States of America

CONTENTS

Baboons are a kind of large monkey. They are very smart animals.

5

Most baboons live in
Africa. Some baboons live
on grasslands. Others live
in woodlands.

Baboons have thick **fur**. Baboon fur can be many colors, such as black, gray, brown, or yellow.

Mother baboons take good care of their babies. A mother baboon most often has one baby at a time.

Mother baboons carry their newborns against their **stomachs**. Older babies ride on their mothers' backs.

Baboons live in groups, called **troops**. Some troops have hundreds of baboons in them.

Baboons make many different sounds to tell other baboons things. They scream, roar, and grunt.

Baboons **groom** troop members with whom they are closest.

Baboons eat many things, such as fruit, grasses, and small animals.

21

Baboons are most often seen on the ground. However, they climb trees to stay out of danger and to sleep at night.

Words to Know

fur

groom

stomach

troop

Index

Web Sites

Due to the changing nature of Internet links, PowerKids Press has developed an online list of Web sites related to the subject of this book. This site is updated regularly. Please use this link to access the list:
www.powerkidslinks.com/safari/baboon/